Quick & Easy Internet Activities for the One-Computer Classroom

U.S. Government

by Jacqueline B. Glasthal

20 Fun, Web-Based Activities
With Reproducible Graphic Organizers That Enable Kids
to Learn the Very Latest Information—On Their Own!

SCHOLASTIC
PROFESSIONAL BOOKS

New York • Toronto • London • Auckland • Sydney
Mexico City • New Dehli • Hong Kong • Buenos Aires

To Mom
and Dad,
Thanks for
helping!

Cover design by **Norma Ortiz**

Interior design by **Holly Grundon**

Interior illustrations by **Mona Mark**

Cover image: Web page used with permission of
Ben's Guide to U.S. Government for Kids

ISBN: 0-439-27858-9

Copyright © 2001 by Jacqueline B. Glasthal

Contents

Using This Book

Welcome to *Quick & Easy Internet Activities for the One-Computer Classroom: U.S. Government!* This collection of 20 Web-based activities will expand your students' knowledge of democracy, the U.S. Constitution, and the three branches of government, while building their Internet research skills at the same time. And what could be a more logical topic for using the World Wide Web? After all, the U.S. government basically invented the Internet by funding a project called ARPAnet in 1969 that allowed scientists, researchers, and government officials to transfer data along high-speed transmission lines. Later this system was expanded and linked to other networks around the world. Thus, the Internet was born!

What's Inside

This book is divided into four chapters: The Basics of Government, A Closer Look at Government, The Politics of Government, and The Business of Government. Each of the 20 activities in this book comes with a teacher page with a step-by-step mini-lesson and extension activity. Reproducible student pages provide simple directions, recording sheets, and graphic organizers that help students complete the activities.

Accessing the Web Sites

In the fast-paced world of the Internet, Web sites can come and go quickly. In addition, since some URLs are quite long and unwieldy, it is easy for students to accidentally type in the wrong address. For these reasons, we decided not to list specific URLs (Uniform Resource Locations, or site addresses) for the activities in this book. Instead, we have published all the necessary links for the activities on our own web site.

To access the Web sites for the activities in this book, go to: **http://www.scholastic.com/profbooks/netexplorations/index.htm**

Click on the book cover for *U.S. Government*. Then, click on the links under each activity name to access the appropriate web sites needed to complete the activity. Remember to bookmark this site or add it to your favorites.

NOTE: You may want to check out the web sites yourself before using them in your classroom. By being familiar with their content, you'll be able to help students navigate through them more efficiently.

Tips for Managing Web-based Activities

The activities in this book require that students spend some time on the computer to do research and complete at least a portion of their worksheets. Whether you have only one computer in your classroom or have access to a computer lab, here are some tips for helping students manage their limited time on the computer effectively:

★ Assign each student or small group about 15 minutes of computer time in rotation. (Most of the activities in this book can be done by students in small groups.) Have the rest of the class complete the non-computer part of the activity, or give them related activities to do while waiting for their turn at the computer.

★ Before students go to the computer, have them read their worksheets carefully so they have a clear, focused idea of what to look for. When they go online, tell students that they don't need to read everything on a site—they can just browse for the information they need and then jot it down on their worksheets.

★ You can hook up your computer to a video monitor or a projector, and have your whole class browse the web together. Students can participate by taking turns clicking the hyperlinks or reading the information.

★ If you don't have online capabilities in your classroom, try offline software, such as Web Whacker (www.bluesquirrel.com), to capture all the pages in a web site and download them. Students can then view the web site from computers that aren't connected to the Internet. You can also save web pages as viewable documents and/or print them out, but they will likely not include pictures and graphics.

More Tips for Smooth Surfing

★ Review with students the basics of using their Internet browsers, such as typing in exact URLs, scrolling, going back and forward between web pages, using hyperlinks, printing, and copying and pasting images.

★ Consider creating "Browser Basics" help sheets or index cards and post them near the computer.

★ Many web sites can contain an overwhelming barrage of information. Encourage students to "browse" the web sites for the information they need, and not worry about reading everything.

Civics Standards

The information and lessons featured in this book meet the following Civics Standards:

Standard 1
Understands ideas about civic life, politics, and government

Standard 2
Understands the essential characteristics of limited and unlimited governments

Standard 4
Understands the concept of a constitution, the various purposes that constitutions serve, and the conditions that contribute to the establishment and maintenance of constitutional government

Standard 5
Understands the major characteristics of systems of shared powers and of parliamentary systems

Standard 6
Understands the advantages and disadvantages of federal, confederal, and unitary systems of government

Standard 8
Understands the central ideas of American constitutional government and how this form of government has shaped the character of American society

Standard 9
Understands the importance of Americans sharing and supporting certain values, beliefs, and principles of American constitutional democracy

Standard 14
Understands issues concerning the disparities between ideals and reality in American political and social life

Standard 15
Understands how the United States Constitution grants and distributes power and responsibilities to national and state government and how it seeks to prevent the abuse of power

Standard 16
Understands the major responsibilities of the national government for domestic and foreign policy, and understands how government is financed through taxation

Standard 17
Understands issues concerning the relationship between state and local governments and the national government and issues pertaining to representation at all three levels of government

Standard 18
Understands the role and importance of law in the American constitutional system and issues regarding the judicial protection of individual rights

Standard 20
Understands the roles of political parties, campaigns, elections, and associations and groups in American politics

Standard 29
Understands the importance of political leadership, public service, and a knowledgeable citizenry in American constitutional democracy

Project Evaluation Form

NAME: _____ DATE: _____

PROJECT: _____

Criteria	Score				
	Poor				Excellent
Follows Directions	1	2	3	4	5
Collaborates with Other Students (*cooperation, flexibility*)	1	2	3	4	5
Uses Computer Time Effectively (*goal-oriented, navigation skill*)	1	2	3	4	5
Curriculum Content (*research, organization, creativity*)	1	2	3	4	5
Writing (*clarity, organization, spelling, grammar*)	1	2	3	4	5
Supporting Visuals (*if applicable*)	1	2	3	4	5

TOTAL SCORE _____

Comments:

_____

_____

_____

_____

Go to: www.scholastic.com/profbooks/netexplorations/index.htm

Social Studies Language Arts Critical Thinking

The Language of Government

Students define five different types of government. They then explain which one they'd most like to rule, why that is, and how they would do so.

BACKGROUND

Does civilization inevitably lead to the establishment of government. And, if so, what type of government works best?

In the 17th century, John Locke believed that people are basically reasonable and tolerant, and thus can get by with very little government. If this is true, *anarchy* (by its most literal definition, "the absence of government") could work in practice.

Thomas Hobbes, however, believed that people are motivated by self-interests. He maintained that people would be willing to give up some individual freedoms if that sacrifice would allow for the security that an organized state could ensure. At the time this theory was controversial in that it suggested that heads of state should rule only by their subjects' consent—an idea now accepted in some countries, but not in others.

DOING THE ACTIVITY

1. Engage students in a discussion about the purposes of government. Ask, What is a government? How many different types of government can you think of? What makes one type of government different from another?

2. Photocopy and distribute page 9 to each student or student pair that will be working at a computer. Have students click on the links at the above web site to help them define the terms in their own words.

3. After completing step 2, have students write about the government they'd create on the back of their worksheets.

ANSWERS:

1. Aristocracy—a government run by those considered to be the best or most able people in the state **2.** Democracy—supreme power is vested in the people and exercised directly by them or by officials they elect **3.** Monarchy—supreme power is lodged in a sovereignty held by a single person **4.** Dictatorship—absolute power is exercised by someone with absolute power or control **5.** Theocracy—a god is recognized as the supreme civil ruler, whose laws are interpreted by ecclesiastical authorities

More To Do:

Defend Your Government!

Take a class poll to determine which form of government was selected most often by students for "their country." Group students by the decisions that they made. Then, after giving these students some time to compare their reasoning, challenge the groups to defend their decisions to others in the class in the form of a debate.

Name(s) _____

Go to: www.scholastic.com/profbooks/netexplorations/index.htm

Start Your Own Government!

Say you could start your own country and run it anyway you want. First, click on the links at the above web site to define the five different types of government below. Next, select the one on which you would base your country's system of government. On the back of this sheet, explain why you selected this type of government and how you would run it.

Types of Government

1. ARISTOCRACY:

_____

_____

_____

_____

2. DEMOCRACY:

_____

_____

_____

_____

3. MONARCHY:

_____

_____

_____

_____

4. DICTATORSHIP:

_____

_____

_____

_____

5. THEOCRACY:

_____

_____

_____

_____

Social Studies
History
Language Arts

Making Compromises as a Nation

Students learn about the United States Constitution by writing a news article about it.

BACKGROUND

To many, the strength of the United States Constitution lies in its flexibility. It arose as a compromise between a national and local system of government, and it remains a document that allows for changes through legislation and amendments. The delegates who took part in the Constitutional Convention represented a wide variety of conflicting opinions and state interests. Their negotiations led to the document—the oldest written national constitution in operation—that still guides our country to this day.

DOING THE ACTIVITY

1. Discuss with students why it is helpful to have written laws. Ask, Who should decide what the written laws should be? How often should they be changed or reevaluated? What should policy makers do when disagreements over the laws arise?

2. Photocopy and distribute page 11 to each student, student pair, or small group com-pleting the activity. Have students click on the links at the above web site to answer the questions on the worksheet.

3. Challenge students to use the information they've collected to write individual news stories about what happened at the Constitutional Convention of 1787.

ANSWERS

1. Philadelphia, Pennsylvania's State House, or Independence Hall, from May to September 1787 **2.** George Washington **3.** Ben Franklin, James Madison, Alexander Hamilton **4.** The biggest issue was whether the federal govern-ment or individual states should have more power, and if larger states should have more power than smaller ones. **5.** The Great Compromise allowed for a "bicameral legisla-ture" made up of a Senate and a House of Representatives. Certain rights were given to the federal government, while other powers were reserved for the states. **6.** The govern-ment could have easily fallen apart, or been vulnerable to a takeover.

More To Do:

Create a Classroom Constitution

Invite students to help create a general set of rules that would help your classroom run more smoothly. Organize students into "committee" groups by topic (such as seating arrangements or keeping the room neat). Invite each committee to suggest specific "Articles" addressing these issues. Then, vote on the document as a class.

Name(s) _____

Go to: www.scholastic.com/profbooks/netexplorations/index.htm

The United States Constitution: In the News!

You're a reporter at the Constitutional Convention—and the United States Constitution is about to be born! Click on the links at the above web site to find out what happened there. Then write a hard-hitting news story about what took place at this historic event.

1. WHERE and WHEN did the Constitutional Convention take place?

_____

_____

2. WHO acted as president of the Constitutional Convention?

_____

_____

3. WHO were some other famous people in attendance?

_____

_____

4. WHAT issues were discussed at the Constitutional Convention?

_____

_____

5. WHAT compromises did the delegates have to make?

_____

_____

6. WHY was it so important for the delegates to find ways to compromise?

_____

_____

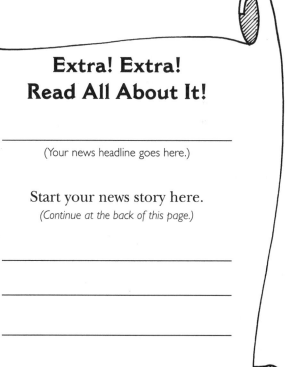

Extra! Extra!
Read All About It!

_____
(Your news headline goes here.)

Start your news story here.
(Continue at the back of this page.)

_____

_____

_____

_____

_____

Go to: www.scholastic.com/profbooks/netexplorations/index.htm

Social
Studies
Art
Critical
Thinking

Norman Rockwell's America

Students learn about Norman Rockwell's Four Freedoms posters, and then create freedom posters of their own.

BACKGROUND

On January 6, 1941, President Franklin D. Roosevelt delivered his historic "Four Freedoms" State of the Union address, urging Congress and American voters to put "patriotism ahead of pocketbooks" and help "make secure . . . a world founded upon four essential human freedoms."

The speech inspired Norman Rockwell to illustrate those freedoms. After his works won public approval when they appeared in the *Saturday Evening Post,* the United States Office of War Information decided to issue them as posters. Sale of the posters raised millions of dollars for the war-bond campaign.

DOING THE ACTIVITY

1. Display reproductions of Norman Rockwell's paintings or books that contain them. (Don't show students copies of *The Four Freedoms* posters yet.)

2. Engage students in a discussion about Rockwell's work. Ask, Approximately when in American history do you think these works were created? How do you think the artist felt about life in the United States?

3. Photocopy and distribute page 13 to each student. Have students click on the links at the above web site to identify the four freedoms that Roosevelt spoke about in his State of the Union address, as illustrated by Rockwell. Then have students write what each of these freedoms means to them.

4. Once everyone has seen the posters, discuss how Rockwell chose to illustrate each freedom. Talk about how else they could have been pictured.

5. After the discussion, encourage students to create their own original posters illustrating one of the freedoms depicted in Rockwell's paintings, or another freedom that they think is important. Have students share their drawings with the rest of the class, explaining in their own words what this particular freedom means to them.

ANSWERS: Freedom of Speech, Freedom of Worship, Freedom from Want, and Freedom from Fear

---

More To Do:

Nothing to Fear But . . .

After students have researched World War II further, invite them to explain, either in discussion or in writing, why President Roosevelt felt that the four freedoms he mentioned in his State of the Union address were at risk in 1941.

Name(s) _____

Go to: www.scholastic.com/profbooks/netexplorations/index.htm

The Four Freedoms

What freedoms did President Franklin D. Roosevelt feel were essential during World War II? Click on the links at this web site and list the four freedoms below, explaining what each one means to you. Then, create a poster showing the freedom that you think is most important and share it with your class!

The Four Freedoms	What This Freedom Means to Me
1.	
2.	
3.	
4.	

Go to: www.scholastic.com/profbooks/netexplorations/index.htm

The U.S. Government "Branches Out"

Students create mobiles representing the three branches of U.S. government and the system of checks and balances they provide.

BACKGROUND

The federal government of the United States consists of three separate but equal branches —the legislative, executive, and judicial. Each branch's basic duties are outlined in the U.S. Constitution: the legislative branch makes laws, the executive branch enforces the laws, and the judicial branch interprets them. Every U.S. citizen participates by helping to elect the officials who take part in this process. Since the responsibilities of each branch of government depend at least in part on decisions of the other two branches, a system of checks and balances is automatically put into place, ensuring that no branch will appropriate more power than the others.

DOING THE ACTIVITY

1. On a board, draw a chart with three columns labeled President, Supreme Court, and Congress. Encourage students to share what they know about each branch of government, and write this information on the board.

2. Photocopy and distribute page 15 to each student or group of three students. (Each group member can focus on one branch of government.) If possible, use a photocopier to enlarge the icons so students will have more space to write.

3. Have students click on the links at the above web site to complete the worksheet. Then, invite them to add any new information they find to the class chart.

4. Provide students with wire hangers and string so that they can complete their balance-of-powers mobiles. Display the completed mobiles in the room.

ANSWERS

The executive branch (president, vice president, and major departments) enforces laws, nominates judges, and can veto bills that Congress has passed. The judicial branch (Supreme Court and inferior courts) interprets laws and determines if laws passed by Congress and/or acts of the executive branch are unconstitutional. The legislative branch (House of Representatives and Senate) makes laws.

More To Do:

Create a Three-Branch Bulletin Board

Using enlarged versions of the icons on the worksheet, invite students to create a bulletin-board display showing a tree with three branches—one for each branch of government. Students can then post news articles related to each aspect of government on the proper "branch" of the tree, after sharing the articles with the class.

Name(s) _____

Go to: www.scholastic.com/profbooks/netexplorations/index.htm

Make a
Balance-of-Powers Mobile!

Click on the links at the above web site to learn about the executive, judicial, and legislative branches of government. On the matching icon below, write the responsibilities of each branch. Then, cut out the icons, tie them to string, and hang them from a wire hanger. Can you balance the three branches of government?

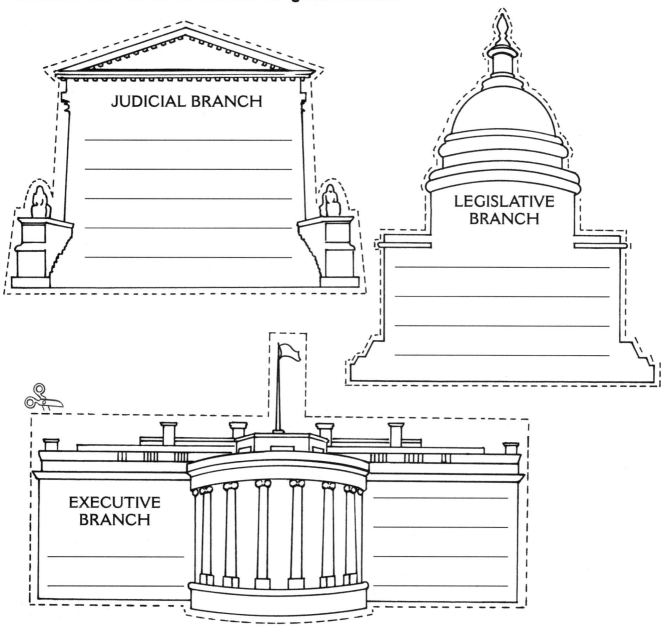

JUDICIAL BRANCH

LEGISLATIVE
BRANCH

EXECUTIVE
BRANCH

Go to: www.scholastic.com/profbooks/netexplorations/index.htm

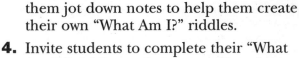

Social Studies Critical Thinking

Symbols of Democracy

Students identify some common symbols associated with United States government before writing their own "What Am I?" riddles about additional symbols.

BACKGROUND

The *Scholastic Children's Dictionary* defines symbol as "a design or an object that represents something else." For example, a small green pine tree on a map symbolizes a forest.

As a country, the United States has many different symbols that have come into being over time. Our nation's flag, for example—one of its predominant symbols—has changed many times in the nation's relatively short history. Before the U.S. declared its independence, the flag was the Union Jack, a symbol of allegiance to England. Later it was the first American flag sewn by Betsy Ross. After the War of 1812, it was the "Star-Spangled Banner," a war-tattered flag still flying free over Fort McHenry.

DOING THE ACTIVITY

1. Ask students, What do you think of when you see the American flag, the Liberty Bell, or the Statue of Liberty? What other symbols do you associate with the United States government, democracy, and/or national pride? List students' responses on the board.

2. Photocopy and distribute page 17 to each student, student pair, or small group.

3. Have students click on the links at the above web site to answer the questions on the worksheet. Then have them jot down notes to help them create their own "What Am I?" riddles.

4. Invite students to complete their "What Am I?" riddles at their seats. Then have them read their own riddles aloud to see if they can stump the rest of the class.

ANSWERS

1. American bald eagle 2. American flag
3. Statue of Liberty 4. Liberty Bell
5. Uncle Sam 6. The White House

More To Do:

Scrapbook of American Symbols

Assign each student one or more of the icons from the list your class has generated. Using whatever research materials are available, instruct students to create an illustrated report giving more historical background about that symbol. When they're done, bind these "American Symbol Reports" into a class scrapbook.

Go to: www.scholastic.com/profbooks/netexplorations/index.htm

I'm an American Symbol...What Am I?

Can you identify each symbol describing itself below? Click on the links at the above web site to help you. Then write your own "What Am I?" riddles about other famous American symbols for friends to solve!

1. I was adopted as the national bird of the United States on June 20, 1782. What am I?

_____

2. My 13 stripes represent the 13 original colonies of the United States. My 50 stars represent the 50 states of the Union. What am I?

_____

3. I was a gift from France to celebrate the 100th birthday of the United States. What am I?

_____

4. The last time I was heard loud and clear was on the anniversary of George Washington's birth in 1846. What am I?

_____

5. Some say that I may be named after Samuel Wilson, a businessman who provided large shipments of meat to the U.S. Army during the War of 1812. But my initials are also the initials of the United States. What am I?

_____

6. I have been the home of every single United States president except George Washington. What am I?

_____

Write Your Own Riddles

Riddle

_____

_____

What am I?
Answer:

_____

Riddle

_____

_____

What am I?
Answer:

_____

Go to: www.scholastic.com/profbooks/netexplorations/index.htm

Social Studies

Who's Running the Country, Anyway?

Students create individual "contact lists" of elected and appointed officials that affect their lives.

BACKGROUND

There are many different types of government in this country. The federal government consists of the three branches that students identified in the activity on pages 14–15. And, though state governments may vary a bit, most reflect the federal government in that they also consist of three branches. Only Nebraska, of all the 50 states, has a *unicameral*, or single, house legislature (as opposed to the more common bicameral system).

Likewise, there is variety in the way that municipal (town or city) governments are run. Alaska, for example, is unique in that most of its landmass is not organized into political subdivisions equivalent to the county form of government. Local government there uses a system of organized boroughs, much like counties in other states. And several areas of the state are not included in any borough because of sparse population. Washington, D.C., represents another unique case, in that it is neither a state nor a territory, yet it has a government that resembles both.

DOING THE ACTIVITY

1. On the board, draw a chart with four columns labeled Federal Government, State Government, County Government, and Municipal Government. Help students to distinguish between these various types.

2. Photocopy and distribute page 19 to each student, student pair, or small group doing the activity. Then, have students click on the links at the above web site to complete the contact list on the worksheet.

More To Do:

So, What Exactly Do They Do?

Invite students to create a glossary explaining the roles of the officials listed on the worksheet, as well as those that students may have added. These could include lieutenant governor, attorney general, secretary of state, comptroller, treasurer, and more. If possible, invite local officials to your school or classroom to speak more about their roles in the government and where they fit in the larger picture.

Name(s) _____

Go to: www.scholastic.com/profbooks/netexplorations/index.htm

Who Ya Gonna Call?

Click on the links at the above web site to find out which people are in charge of your government these days, and how you can contact them. Write the names of the government officials and their contact information in the spaces below. Continue at the back of this page for your local officials.

Federal Government

Who	How to Contact
President	Phone Address E-mail
Vice President	Phone Address E-mail
My Senators *	Phone Address E-mail
My Local Representative	Phone Address E-mail

* If you live in the District of Columbia, this category does not apply.

State Government

Governor	Phone Address E-mail

Go to: www.scholastic.com/profbooks/netexplorations/index.htm

Social Studies Careers

President for Hire

Students create a "Help Wanted" ad for president of the United States.

BACKGROUND

On being president, John F. Kennedy once said, "The pay is good and I can walk to work." But there is, obviously, much more to the job than that.

George Washington, for one, didn't even want to be president—a fact that some say actually helped him to win! After gaining their independence from England's King George III, Americans did not want another power-hungry leader. In 1789 and 1792, Washington became the only president to be elected unanimously by the Electoral College.

Washington also set the precedent for a two-term presidency. All other presidents followed his lead until Franklin D. Roosevelt successfully ran for office four times. Six years after Roosevelt's death, Congress passed the 22nd Amendment to the Constitution, limiting the president to a maximum of two terms.

DOING THE ACTIVITY

1. Discuss with students the qualities or characteristics they'd like to see in a president of the United States. Ask, Who do you think have been some of

this country's greatest presidents? What makes them stand out in your mind as great leaders? What other traits do you think a president should have?

2. Photocopy and distribute page 21 to each student, student pair, or small group. Have students click on the links at the above web site to complete the worksheet.

3. Once the worksheets are completed, go over the answers as a class. Ask students if they would want to change or update any of these "job qualifications" if they had the opportunity. If so, which ones and why? If not, why do students think these specific restrictions make sense?

ANSWERS

1. 35 2. the United States 3. 14
4. Washington, D.C. 5. 4 6. 8
7. Answers will vary 8. Answers will vary
9. Approximately $390,000 a year, plus a $50,000 expense account

---

More To Do:

Does the Electoral College Work?

The 2000 presidential election refueled a debate that goes far back in U.S. history over whether or not the Electoral College system works. In 1876, Rutherford B. Hayes did not receive the most popular votes, but won the majority of electoral votes, and thus the election. Organize students into two teams and invite them to debate the pros and cons of the Electoral College system.

Name(s) _____

Go to: www.scholastic.com/profbooks/netexplorations/index.htm

Help Wanted:
President of the United States

Know anyone who'd make a great president of the United States? Click on the links at the above web site to help you fill in the blank spaces in the "Help Wanted" ad below. As you search for the answers, think about whether or not you agree that these are good qualifications for a United States president to have.

MUST BE:

HELP WANTED:
PRESIDENT OF THE UNITED STATES

1. at least _____ years old.

2. a natural-born citizen

   of _____.

3. a resident of the United States at least _____ years before applying.

4. willing to relocate to _____.

5. willing to serve for a minimum of _____ years.

6. willing to accept that he or she will not serve for more than _____ years.

7. The right candidate will _____

   _____.

8. Responsibilities include _____

   _____.

9. SALARY: _____ annually, plus _____

Go to: www.scholastic.com/profbooks/netexplorations/index.htm

Social
Studies
History

The Buck Stopped With Them

Students use facts gathered about various presidents to identify each one.

BACKGROUND

On his desk, President Harry Truman kept a sign that read "The Buck Stops Here," indicating that he was willing to take responsibility for the actions of his administration. And that he did—particularly after making the controversial decision to drop the first atomic bomb ever used in warfare on August 6, 1945.

Whether he likes it or not, rarely (if ever) has a president found a way to "pass the buck" and escape the scrutiny of historians and public opinion. No matter how calm or turbulent the times in which each president leads, and no matter how long or short the administration, each president is inevitably destined to be judged by both contemporaries and future generations.

DOING THE ACTIVITY

1. Ask students, Who is currently the President of the United States? Which other presidents can you name? What crucial events or actions in United States history is each one associated with? Would you ever want the responsibilities of being president of the United States? Why or why not?

2. Photocopy and distribute page 23 to each student. Have students click on the links at the above web site to complete the worksheet.

ANSWERS
1. Andrew Jackson **2.** Grover Cleveland **3.** Theodore Roosevelt **4.** Franklin D. Roosevelt **5.** Harry S Truman **6.** John F. Kennedy **7.** Lyndon Johnson **8.** Richard Nixon

---

More To Do:

And If I Am Elected . . .

Invite students to select a president from history and, based on that president's actual accomplishments, write a speech that president might have given before he was elected, promising what he would do while in office.

Name(s) _____

Go to: www.scholastic.com/profbooks/netexplorations/index.htm

Leaders of the Pack

How did these eight U.S. presidents change the United States—and the world? Click on the links at the above web site to learn more about them. Then identify each one, as described below.

Richard Nixon	**Lyndon Johnson**	**Grover Cleveland**
Franklin Delano Roosevelt	**John F. Kennedy**	**Harry S Truman**
Theodore Roosevelt		**Andrew Jackson**

1. I laid the foundation for America's modern economy. I was also the only President to pay off the national debt and leave office with a surplus in the United States Treasury. WHO AM I?

_____

2. I vetoed Congress about 600 times. Many of these vetoes were of pension bills for undeserving Civil War veterans, who claimed to have been injured in the war—but hadn't been! WHO AM I?

_____

3. I protected large amounts of the nation's wilderness, preserving about 200,000 acres of government land, mostly in the form of national parks and wildlife refuges. WHO AM I?

_____

4. In an effort to lift the United States out of the "Great Depression," I created "New Deal" legislation during my first 100 days in office, giving jobs to millions of Americans. WHO AM I?

_____

5. I approved the use of atomic weapons on Hiroshima and Nagasaki, Japan, to help end World War II. Later, I joined other nations to form NATO, a military alliance to protect Western nations against communism. WHO AM I?

_____

6. I was the youngest U.S. president ever elected to office—and the youngest to die in office. I created the Peace Corps in which Americans help people of developing countries. I also negotiated the first nuclear weapons treaty in history. WHO AM I?

_____

7. I signed into law more than 200 pieces of major legislation, including a billion-dollar anti-poverty program and a groundbreaking civil rights bill. I also developed Medicaid and Medicare to help poor and elderly people pay their medical bills. WHO AM I?

_____

8. I was the first U.S. president to visit and establish diplomatic relations with communist China and to negotiate an arms-control treaty with the Soviet Union. I was also the first to resign from office. This happened after I was accused of involvement in a scandal known as "Watergate." WHO AM I?

_____

Go to: www.scholastic.com/profbooks/netexplorations/index.htm

Social Studies Critical Thinking

Pick Your Presidential Cabinet!

Students imagine that they are the president of the United States and determine which member of their cabinet to consult on a number of issues.

BACKGROUND

Since the days of George Washington, presidents have been handpicking appointed officers of the cabinet, who must then be approved by two-thirds of the Senate. Washington's first cabinet was made up of four people: a secretary of state, secretary of the treasury, secretary of war, and attorney general, plus his chief of staff.

George W. Bush's cabinet, in comparison, includes the heads of 14 "statutory" cabinet-level departments (which students will identify in this activity), the Vice President, and the heads of three other "discretionary" agencies that he determined should be a part of his cabinet.

DOING THE ACTIVITY

1. Ask students to suggest people that they might want to turn to for advice if they were president of the United States. Once you've generated some ideas, inform students that this is exactly what the president's cabinet was created to do.

2. Photocopy and distribute page 25 to each student pair or small group. Have students click on the links at the above web site to complete the first part of the worksheet.

3. After they've returned to their seats, have students complete the rest of the worksheet. If available, allow students to consult newspapers, newsmagazines, and/or history textbooks for ideas.

ANSWERS

1. Department of Agriculture 2. Department of Commerce 3. Department of Defense 4. Department of Education 5. Department of Energy 6. Department of Health and Human Services 7. Department of Housing and Urban Development 8. Department of the Interior 9. Department of Justice (headed by the attorney general) 10. Department of Labor 11. Department of State 12. Department of Transportation 13. Department of the Treasury 14. Department of Veteran Affairs

---

More To Do:

Is Anybody Missing?

Point out to students that the number of cabinet members generally has increased over time. Invite them to suggest additional agencies that may be needed in the future. (For example, think about advances being made in science and technology.) Then, ask students to discuss whether or not there could be too many advisors.

Name(s) _____

Go to: www.scholastic.com/profbooks/netexplorations/index.htm

Don't Go It Alone!

You've just been elected president of the United States. But that means you've got problems to overcome and national dilemmas to solve. Don't go it alone! That's what members of your cabinet are for! The president's official cabinet is made up of the heads of 14 federal agencies. Click on the links at the above web site to find out what these agencies are, and write them below.

1. _____   8. _____

2. _____   9. _____

3. _____   10. _____

4. _____   11. _____

5. _____   12. _____

6. _____   13. _____

7. _____   14. _____

Now, think of one or more issues that you, as the president, might want to consult your cabinet about. Describe the situation here, continuing on the back of this page, if necessary.

_____

_____

Decide which cabinet member(s) you think might be most helpful to you in the situation you described above. List each one(s) and explain why on the lines below, continuing at the back of this page, if necessary.

_____

_____

Go to: www.scholastic.com/profbooks/netexplorations/index.htm

Social Studies

Comparing the House and the Senate

Students complete a Venn diagram in which they identify the distinct responsibilities of the Senate and the House of Representatives, as well as those duties shared by both.

BACKGROUND

One particularly thorny issue for the delegates at the Constitutional Convention of 1787 was trying to determine whether all of the states should be treated equally in the new government (that is, whether each state was entitled to one vote), or whether those that were larger and had more people were entitled to have "a louder say."

Finally, everyone agreed to organize a Congress made up of two "houses," or parts. In the Senate each state would be equally represented by two Senators. But in the House of Representatives, representation would be based on population. The more people living in a particular state, the more representatives that state would be allotted. Thus, the "Great Compromise" was born.

DOING THE ACTIVITY

1. Remind students that the United States Congress is made up of two distinct bodies: the U.S. Senate and the House of Representatives. Encourage students to share what they know about each of these, making sure that they are aware of the facts provided in the background information.

2. Photocopy and distribute page 27 to each student or group of three students. (One group member can focus on the responsibilities of the Senate, another on the House of Representatives, and the third on their shared responsibilities.) Have students click on the links at the above web site to complete the worksheet.

ANSWERS

Both houses of Congress share the responsibilities of approving all laws necessary for the operation of the government, making the decision to declare war, maintaining the armed forces, assessing taxes, borrowing money, minting currency, and regulating commerce. Individual responsibilities of the House of Representatives and the Senate include all of these and more.

More To Do:

How Does Congress Affect Our Lives?

Have students work in groups to research different aspects of American culture—from agriculture and auto safety, to school lunches and voting rights. Have each group find out how congressional decisions about these issues have affected life in America, and have them report back to the rest of the class on what they learn.

Name(s) _____

Go to: www.scholastic.com/profbooks/netexplorations/index.htm

Ring Around the Congress

Click on the links at the above web site to learn about the United States Senate and the House of Representatives. Then, record the jobs of the United States Senate and House of Representatives and the jobs that both houses share in the Venn diagram below.

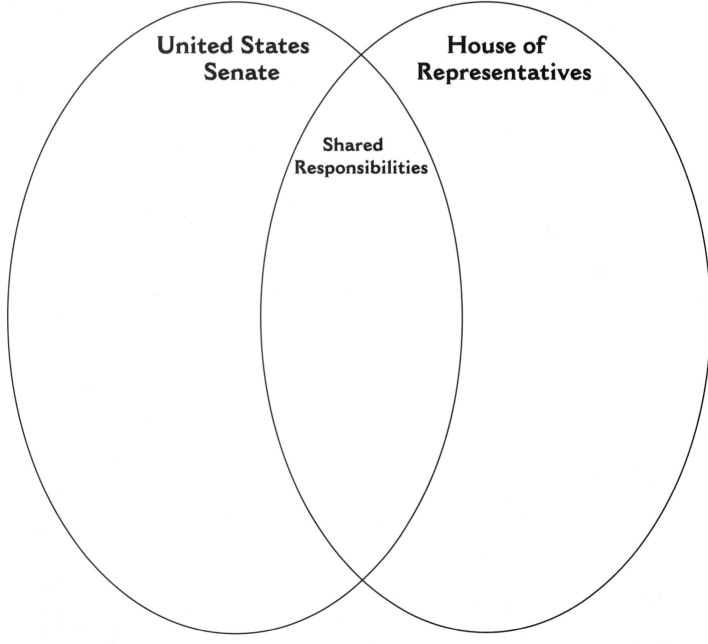

United States Senate

House of Representatives

Shared Responsibilities

Go to: www.scholastic.com/profbooks/netexplorations/index.htm

Social Studies History

How Much Power Does Congress Have?

Students order a series of events to find out how the Supreme Court's right of judicial review was established.

BACKGROUND

Thomas Jefferson, the nation's third president, was also the first who did not consider himself a Federalist—someone who believes in a strong federal government. So, when he came into office, many of the nation's judges, who had all been appointed by his predecessors, were Federalists. And, before his term was up, "lame-duck" President John Adams would attempt to appoint even more.

Many of these appointments were not delivered, however, by the time Jefferson was sworn into office. So William Marbury, one of the appointees, went to the Supreme Court, asking that his appointment be made. In deciding the outcome of the case, the Supreme Court declared that the Judiciary Act of 1789, under which the appointments were created, was unconstitutional. Because of this decision, Marbury never was made a justice. But his name did go down in legal

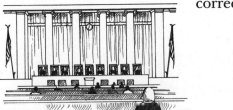

history. It was with this case that the Supreme Court's power of judicial review —the right to declare acts of Congress unconstitutional—was established.

DOING THE ACTIVITY

1. Review the responsibilities of the three branches of government, focusing on those of the Supreme Court. Point out to students that the primary role of the Supreme Court is to make sure that actions of the other two branches remain true to the U.S. Constitution.

2. Photocopy and distribute page 29 to each student, student pair, or small group. Have students click on the links at the above web site to put the events on the worksheet in the correct order.

ANSWERS
A. 5 **B.** 3 **C.** 4 **D.** 2
E. 7 **F.** 1 **G.** 6

More To Do:

What Would Marbury Have to Say?

Despite his role in the annals of history, William Marbury was still quite disappointed that he never received his commission as a justice of the peace after Thomas Jefferson took office. Working from his perspective, invite students to write a speech in which they argue against the Supreme Court ruling on Marbury's behalf.

Name(s) _____

Go to: www.scholastic.com/profbooks/netexplorations/index.htm

The Case of
Marbury vs. Madison

What series of events led to the Supreme Court exercising its right to review the actions of Congress for the first time? Click on the links at the above web site to help you put the following events in correct order. Use "1" to indicate the first event that occurred, "2" for the second event, and so on.

_____ **A.** John Marshall, in his new position as chief justice of the Supreme Court, declares that James Madison should have given Marbury his commission under the Judiciary Act of 1789. However, in the same court decision, he states that part of the Judiciary Act of 1789 is unconstitutional, and therefore need not be followed.

_____ **B.** Newly elected President Thomas Jefferson refuses to honor the judicial appointments of his predecessor, John Adams.

_____ **C.** William Marbury, one of John Adams' judicial appointees, sues Secretary of State James Madison in an attempt to force him to deliver his commission as a justice of the peace.

_____ **D.** On his last days in office, John Adams' judicial appointees are confirmed by the United States Senate.

_____ **E.** Warren Burger, who served as a chief justice of the United States Supreme Court between 1969 and 1986, hangs a portrait of William Marbury in the chambers of the United States Supreme Court, right beside a portrait of James Madison—the man who refused to grant him the position that he sought.

_____ **F.** After losing the presidential election of 1800, but before he leaves office, President John Adams appoints a number of judges from his political party into office.

_____ **G.** In 1857, more than 50 years after the case of *Marbury vs. Madison* was determined, the Supreme Court declares another act of Congress unconstitutional—this time it was the Dred Scott decision. Though it has used this power of "judicial review" sparingly, the Supreme Court is still the final word in interpreting the U.S. Constitution.

Quick & Easy Internet Activities: U.S. Government **29**

Go to: www.scholastic.com/profbooks/netexplorations/index.htm

Social Studies History Critical Thinking

Can the Supreme Court Change Its Mind?

Students find out how Supreme Court cases, such as the famous *Brown vs. Board of Education,* are decided, and how they can impact people's daily lives.

BACKGROUND

U.S. Supreme Court justices, once appointed, hold that position for life, unless found guilty of wrongdoing. This provision allows them to decide cases on the basis of conscience without fear of political repercussions. Otherwise, controversial decisions, such as the one made by the court in *Brown vs. Board of Education* may never have come to pass.

As it was, conflicts over civil rights issues had been plaguing the United States since it was established. They were a source of friction in the writing of the Constitution, and further divided the country during the Civil War. And, though the *Brown vs. Board of Education* decision was unanimous in the Supreme Court, it was not easily accepted by all citizens. Many Southern politicians charged the court with a "clear abuse of judicial power." Even 10 years after the case was decided, only one percent of African-American students in the South attended desegregated schools.

DOING THE ACTIVITY

1. Ask students if they have ever heard the phrase "separate but equal." What do they think it means? Can they think of examples of situations in which people might be kept separate from other groups, yet feel confident that they will be treated equally? Why or why not?

2. Photocopy and distribute page 31 to each student pair or group. Have students click on the links at the above web site to answer the questions.

ANSWERS

1. If an 1890 Louisiana statute mandating racially segregated but equal public facilities (i.e., railroad carriages) violated the equal protection clause of the 14th Amendment to the U.S. Constitution **2.** The Supreme Court ruled that "separate but equal" laws did not imply the inferiority of one race to another. **3.** If segregating children in public schools violated the equal protection clause of the 14th Amendment **4.** The court determined that "separate but equal" laws are unequal, and thus violate people's constitutional rights. **5** and **6.** Answers will vary.

More To Do:

Just "De Factos," Ma'am

The Supreme Court's *Brown vs. Board of Education* decision brought an end to "de jure," or legally imposed, segregation. However, many believe that "de facto" segregation— or segregation in fact—still exists. Encourage students to provide examples of "de jure" and "de facto" segregation, and list them on a chart.

Name(s) _____

Go to: www.scholastic.com/profbooks/netexplorations/index.htm

You Be the Judge!

The job of the United States Supreme Court is to interpret the Constitution. But what if their interpretation changes? Click on the links at the above web site to answer these questions. Continue at the back of this page if necessary.

1. What was the United States Supreme Court asked to decide in the 1896 court case *Plessy vs. Ferguson?*

_____

_____

2. How did the United States Supreme Court rule in the 1896 court case *Plessy vs. Ferguson?*

_____

_____

3. What was the United States Supreme Court asked to decide in the 1954 court case *Brown vs. Board of Education?*

_____

_____

4. How did the United States Supreme Court rule in the 1954 court case *Brown vs. Board of Education?*

_____

_____

5. Now you be the judge! The Supreme Court members based their unanimous 1954 decision on their interpretation of the 14th Amendment to the U.S. Constitution. Read this amendment, then explain how they might have interpreted it to make their case.

_____

_____

6. Would you have agreed with the other Supreme Court justices if you had served on the court back in 1954? Why or why not? Explain your answer at the back of this page.

Go to: www.scholastic.com/profbooks/netexplorations/index.htm

Social Studies Critical Thinking

Federal vs. State Rights

Students distinguish between powers shared by the national and state governments from those reserved for each.

BACKGROUND

Some countries, like France and England, have a strong centralized government, that is, the national government maintains all the power. The American government, when it was first founded, was just the opposite. The 13 colonies, which had been ruled by England, insisted that the state governments remain strong. Over time, however, they realized that they could not survive as a country unless the national government was instilled with some basic powers. A balance needed to be reached. That's how our current federal system—one in which power is shared between the national government and the states—arose.

DOING THE ACTIVITY

1. On the board, draw a chart with two columns labeled Federal Government and State Government. Encourage students to share what they know about each. Ask, Why do you think car theft is handled under state law, but transporting a stolen car across state lines becomes a national issue? What responsibilities do you think the states and national government should share?

2. Photocopy and distribute page 33 to each student or group of three students. (One group member can focus on the responsibilities of the federal government, another on state governments, and the third on their shared responsibilities.) Have students click on the links at the above web site to complete the worksheet.

3. Go over the worksheet as a class. To test students' comprehension of what they've read, ask questions such as, Is a state, such as Nevada or Maine, allowed to make a treaty with another country, like France or Germany, on its own? Why or why not? Which has the right to tax citizens: the national government, state governments, or both? What did you learn that you found particularly interesting or surprising?

ANSWERS
1. N **2.** T **3.** L **4.** G **5.** A **6.** O
7. U **8.** I **9.** D **10.** R.
Bonus: NATIONAL GUARD

More To Do:

It's Our Right!

Divide the class into two teams, one representing the national government, the other a state in the Union. Have the state team begin by calling out a right reserved for the states. The national government team should respond with a right reserved for the federal government. When a team can no longer think of a response, that team loses.

Name(s) _____

Go to: www.scholastic.com/profbooks/netexplorations/index.htm

We've Got the Power!

Click on the links at the above web site to learn about the limited powers of both our state and national governments. Answer the questions below, circling the letter of correct answers to identify the oldest fighting force in the United States.

1. **To which of the following do all adults pay taxes?**

   Q. state government   R. national government   N. both

2. **Which is responsible for setting up the polls on Election Day?**

   T. state government   U. national government   F. both

3. **To which of the following would another country go if it wanted the United States to help it protect its borders from foreign attacks?**

   B. state government   L. national government   S. both

4. **Which gets the money you pay when you purchase postage stamps?**

   I. state government   G. national government   W. both

5. **Which has a larger say in what students learn in school?**

   A. state government   E. national government   U. both

6. **Which has the right to create laws, as long as they don't conflict with the Constitution?**

   K. state government   P. national government   O. both

7. **Which decides if companies are overpolluting the air and water?**

   Y. state government   U. national government   M. both

8. **Which determines how old someone needs to be before he or she can drive?**

   I. state government   J. national government   K. both

9. **Which determines how old someone needs to be before he or she can vote?**

   E. state government   D. national government   G. both

10. **Which must create a budget, showing how much money they plan to spend during the coming year?**

   O. state government   C. national government   R. both

In colonial days, local militia units were created to protect citizens from invasions, such as Indian attacks. Write the letter of your circled answers on the line with the matching question number below to find out what name local militia units of the U.S. Armed Forced go by today:

____ ____ ____ ____ ____ ____ ____ ____   ____ ____ ____ ____ ____

1   5   2   8   6   1   5   3   4   7   5   10   9

Go to: www.scholastic.com/profbooks/netexplorations/index.htm

Social Studies
Critical Thinking

What a Political Party!

Students describe the basic platforms of five political parties before creating their own unique political party platform.

BACKGROUND

America's founding fathers, particularly George Washington, were strongly opposed to political parties, and nothing is said about them in the U.S. Constitution. Nevertheless, they have been a basic element of United States government as far back as Washington's day. The platforms of the original two parties —the Federalists and the Anti-Federalists— centered around the issue of whether or not there should be a strong centralized government in the newly formed nation.

To some extent this debate still goes on between Republicans and Democrats. The Democrats advocate a "reinvented" form of government and the Republicans promote the cause of state rights. And, though most third-party candidates have failed to get elected, promoters of third-party platforms can influence legislation and basic policy decisions as well.

DOING THE ACTIVITY

1. Assess what students already know about political parties in the United States. Ask, What is a political party? What is a political

party platform? Can you name some political parties that exist in America today? What were some of the first political parties in United States history?

2. Photocopy and distribute page 35 to each student or student pair. Using the links at the above web site, have students complete the worksheet.

3. Go over the worksheet answers as a class. Be sure to leave time for each student or student pair to make a case for their own political party platform. To confirm student understanding, continue the earlier discussion with questions like, In what ways do you find these party platforms to be similar? How do they differ from one another? How would you describe the language of most of these platforms? Why do you think this is? Did you find yourself using similar language in your own party platform? Why or why not?

ANSWERS

Answers will vary, and party platforms may change somewhat every four years.

More To Do:

Makes Good Horse Sense To Me . . .

After researching the history of the donkey and the elephant as symbols of the Democratic and Republican parties, respectively, invite students to suggest animals that might best represent the other political parties listed. Have them draw these icons and explain why each of these animals is an appropriate "mascot" for the party.

Name(s) _____

Go to: www.scholastic.com/profbooks/netexplorations/index.htm

Have You Got a Platform to Stand On?

Every political party in the United States is associated with certain beliefs, known as that party's platform. Discover the basic platforms of the five political parties listed below using the links at the above web site. Then build a platform of your own!

Political Party	Platform
Democratic	
Republican	
Libertarian	
Green Party	
Communist	

Now make up a name for your own new political party and explain its platform on the back of this page.

Go to: www.scholastic.com/profbooks/netexplorations/index.htm

Social Studies
History
Critical Thinking

The Bill of Rights

Students complete a self-checking puzzle
in which they learn more about the Bill of Rights.

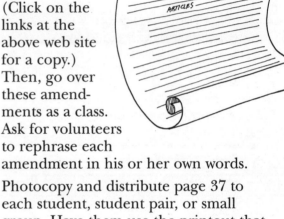

BACKGROUND

It was not until 1791, four years after the United States Constitution was completed and made public, that a Bill of Rights was adopted. These first ten amendments to the Constitution were cause for controversy at the time. Some states only agreed to ratify the Constitution with the understanding that a Bill of Rights would later be added. But many Federalists argued that such a bill was not needed. Obviously they were over-ruled. Although a 12-amendment Bill of Rights was originally proposed, two of these amendments were not approved by three-fourths of the state legislature. The remaining ten, however, are what we know today as the Bill of Rights.

DOING THE ACTIVITY

1. Open a discussion by asking students if they know what an amendment is. *(A change made to a law or legal document)* By what other name are the first ten amendments to the United States Constitution called? *(The Bill of Rights)*

2. After discussing the history of the Bill of Rights, print out and distribute a copy of it for each student. (Click on the links at the above web site for a copy.) Then, go over these amendments as a class. Ask for volunteers to rephrase each amendment in his or her own words.

3. Photocopy and distribute page 37 to each student, student pair, or small group. Have them use the printout that you distributed or click on the links at the above web site to help them complete the activity.

ANSWERS
A. Sixth **B.** First **C.** Fifth **D.** Eighth
E. Second **F.** Third **G.** Tenth
H. Seventh **I.** Ninth **J.** Fourth
Riddle Answer: Odor in the court!

More To Do:

Rock the Constitution!

After researching the history of a particular amendment to the Constitution, invite each student to create a rap song explaining what that amendment says, and how it came to be.

Name(s) _____

Go to: www.scholastic.com/profbooks/netexplorations/index.htm

Know Your Rights!

The first ten amendments to the United States Constitution are known as the Bill of Rights. What freedoms do they give you? Use a copy of the Bill of Rights to help you answer these questions. For each answer, spell out the amendment's order number (i.e., first, second, third). To find the answer to the riddle at the bottom of the page, write the letters on the corresponding numbered lines below.

Which amendment . . .

A. gives you the right to call a lawyer if you are accused of a crime?

___ ___ ___ ___
     1

B. allows you to protest in public against a law with which you disagree?

___ ___ ___ ___ ___
     8

C. guarantees that people need not testify against themselves in court if they are accused of a crime?

___ ___ ___ ___ ___
     11

D. denies a police officer the right to injure a person charged of a crime except, perhaps, in self-defense?

___ ___ ___ ___ ___ ___
     5

E. guarantees that each member of the militia, or National Guard, will be allowed to carry weapons in order to protect his or her country?

___ ___ ___ ___ ___ ___
  6 3

F. exists because, during the American Revolution, British soldiers were given the right by the Crown to stay in the house of any colonists that they chose?

___ ___ ___ ___ ___
    4 9

G. entitles states to create their own laws, as long as they don't conflict with the U.S. Constitution?

___ ___ ___ ___ ___
    10

H. says that people accused of a crime are entitled to be judged by a jury?

___ ___ ___ ___ ___
    12

I. says that just because a right isn't specifically stated in the U.S. Constitution, this doesn't mean that you don't have it?

___ ___ ___ ___
    2

J. says that police officers may not search your house unless they first obtain a warrant?

___ ___ ___ ___ ___
  7 13

RIDDLE:

What did the Supreme Court justice say when a skunk walked in the courtroom?

___ ___ ___ ___ ___ ___ ___ ___ ___ ___ ___ ___ ___ ___!
 7 9 3 8   2 10   1 11 12   6 7 13 4 5

Go to: www.scholastic.com/profbooks/netexplorations/index.htm

Social
Studies
History
Critical
Thinking

Making Amendments

Students identify actual amendments to the U.S. Constitution from a list that includes some that have failed to pass.

BACKGROUND

Only one Constitutional amendment—the 18th, legalizing prohibition in 1919—has ever been repealed, or canceled. This occurred 14 years after it was ratified, with the passage of the 21st Amendment in 1933.

Before an amendment can be added to the Constitution, two-thirds of the Congress and three-quarters of the state legislatures must agree to it. Obtaining that many approvals is no easy process. It's no wonder that, out of the thousands of amendments that have been proposed, only 27 have ever been approved.

DOING THE ACTIVITY

1. Engage students in a discussion regarding similarities and differences between a Constitutional amendment and other forms of legislation. Ask, How many amendments are there to the United States Constitution? *(27)* What makes these amendments different from other types of laws? *(Amendments are much more difficult to pass, or ratify, and are equally difficult to repeal. They are, in general, more open-ended than other laws and thus subject to the interpretations of the times in which they are used.)* When do you think a Constitutional amendment should be passed as opposed to another kind of law?

2. Photocopy and distribute page 39 to each student or student pair. Have them click on the links at the above web site to complete the activity.

3. Go over the worksheet answers as a class. Continue the earlier discussion with questions such as, Given what you now know, why do you think some of the proposed amendments failed to pass? Do you think any of these should be added as amendments to the Constitution? If so, which ones and why? Are there any actual amendments on the list that you think are unnecessary? If so, which ones and why? If not, why do you think that they are all important?

ANSWERS
C. 24 **G.** 13 **M.** NA **R.** NA **O.** NA
E. 26 **E.** 15 **E.** NA **E.** 22 **R.** 19
Bonus: Greece and Rome

More To Do:

Amendment Bingo

Create a Bingo-like 5-by-5 grid game card for each student. Randomly place the Roman numerals I (1) to XXVII (27) on each card. As you call out rights granted by various Constitutional amendments, students cover the matching amendment numerals with game pieces. The first player to correctly cover five amendment numerals in a row wins.

Name(s) _____

Go to: www.scholastic.com/profbooks/netexplorations/index.htm

Pass the Amendment, Please!

To date, more than 11,000 amendments to the United States Constitution have been introduced into Congress. But, of these, only 27 have actually been passed! Click on the links at the above web site to find out which of the statements below are actual Constitutional amendments. Write the amendment's number in the space next to the true statements. Write "NA" (non-amendment) in the space next to the statements that are not true.

_____ **C.** No citizen will be denied the right to vote because he or she hasn't paid taxes.

_____ **G.** Slavery is forbidden throughout the United States.

_____ **M.** It is illegal to burn or otherwise damage a United States flag.

_____ **R.** The federal government must find a way to balance the national budget.

_____ **O.** No member of the U.S. Senate or U.S. House of Representatives will serve more than a 12-year term in office.

_____ **E.** All U.S. citizens must be 18 or older before they can vote in a national election.

_____ **E.** United States citizens have the right to vote, no matter what their race or color.

_____ **E.** Citizens of the United States will directly elect their president, rather than use the electoral college system.

_____ **E.** No President will serve more than two terms in office.

_____ **R.** United States citizens have the right to vote, whether they are male or female.

Fun Fact:

The designers of Washington, D.C., wanted the city to reflect the ancient civilizations upon which its system of government is based. To find out the first civilization, unscramble the letters next to the actual amendments. Then unscramble the letters next to the NAs to find out the second one.

The buildings of Washington, D.C., were built to resemble the ancient buildings of

____ ____ ____ ____ ____ ____ **and** ____ ____ ____ ____

Go to: www.scholastic.com/profbooks/netexplorations/index.htm

Social Studies Critical Thinking

A Bill on Capitol Hill

Students complete a flow chart to find out what steps need to be taken before a bill can be made into a law.

BACKGROUND

Given the process that a bill must go through before it is made into a law, it is somewhat amazing that new laws are ever passed! Somehow, though, they are—often after much debate, research, and often modification and rephrasing by both houses of Congress.

DOING THE ACTIVITY

1. Direct students to the links at the about web site to read about the steps involved in how a bill becomes a law.

2. Photocopy and distribute page 41 to each student, student pair, or small group. Provide extra sheets of paper, plus glue or tape, in the work area.

3. When everyone has had a chance to complete the activity, go over it as a class. If possible, make an enlargement of the puzzle pieces and invite students to pin them up on the bulletin board in the correct arrangement to complete the flow chart. Students can then use this enlarged model to check their own work.

ANSWERS

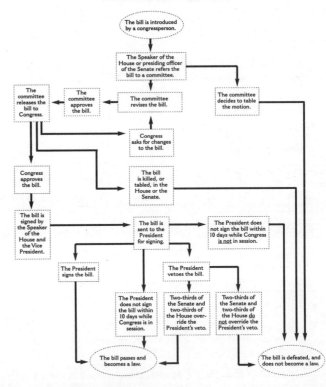

HOW A BILL BECOMES A LAW

More To Do:

Act It Out!

Simulate the process of how a bill becomes a law in the classroom: Create signs showing the various hands a bill must pass through before it becomes a law (Speaker of the House, presiding officer of the Senate, Senate committee, etc.). Distribute these to various students and position them strategically throughout the room. Select one student to be the actual bill itself, and have him or her visit—in correct sequence— the players necessary for the bill to pass.

Name(s) _____

Go to: www.scholastic.com/profbooks/netexplorations/index.htm

There Oughtta Be a Law!

What does it take for a bill to be made into a law? Click on the links at the above web site to learn more about each step. Cut out the shapes below and use them with arrows to create a flow chart showing the process that a bill goes through before it becomes a law. Tape or glue your flow chart on a separate page.

HOW A BILL BECOMES A LAW

The bill is introduced by a congressperson.

The President does not sign the bill within 10 days while Congress is in session.

The committee releases the bill to Congress.

The bill is signed by the Speaker of the House and the Vice President.

The committee decides to table the motion.

The bill is sent to the President for signing.

Two-thirds of the Senate and two-thirds of the House override the President's veto.

Congress asks for changes to the bill.

Congress approves the bill.

The bill passes and becomes a law.

The bill is killed, or tabled, in the House or the Senate.

The committee approves the bill.

The committee revises the bill.

Two-thirds of the Senate and two-thirds of the House do not override the President's veto.

The President vetoes the bill.

The President signs the bill.

The Speaker of the House or presiding officer of the Senate refers the bill to a committee.

The bill is defeated, and does not become a law.

The President does not sign the bill within 10 days while Congress is not in session.

Go to: www.scholastic.com/profbooks/netexplorations/index.htm

Who's Footing the Bill? State vs. Federal Taxes

Students distinguish between items that are paid for by their federal, state, and local governments.

BACKGROUND

State, federal, and local taxes are collected in many different ways. Federal and state governments get much of their money from income taxes, but they also collect employment taxes on wages, sales tax on many goods and services, and excise taxes on specific items like tobacco, alcohol, gasoline, and telephone services. Federal and state governments often provide local governments with tax revenue for schools, highways, and other services. Their primary source of revenue, however, tends to be local property taxes supplemented by money from parking meters, fines, construction and recreation permits, lotteries, and other local fees.

DOING THE ACTIVITY

1. On the board, create a chart with three columns labeled Federal, State, and Local. Ask students to suggest services that they think are paid for by tax dollars. Prompt them with questions such as, Who pays for firefighters? Who pays to set up the polls on election day? What about the textbooks that are used in public schools? Write students' answers in the appropriate columns. If there is a disagreement, jot down the service in any and all columns that students suggest.

2. Photocopy and distribute page 43 to each student, student pair, or small group. Go over any terms on the worksheet that students might not be familiar with. Then, have students click on the links at the above web site to complete the activity.

3. Go over the worksheet answers as a class. Then revisit the chart that you and your students created on the board. Have students help you make corrections, if necessary.

ANSWERS

FEDERAL: Interest payments on the national debt, medical care for disabled veterans, salary of air-traffic controllers, funding for medical research **STATE:** Salary for Motor Vehicle Bureau employees, scholarship dollars for state-university students, salary for bridge and tunnel toll collectors, salary for highway patrol officers **LOCAL:** 3 new school buses, 1 new bulb for the street light on Main Street, 5 new library books for the public library, food and clothing for prisoners at the county jail.

More To Do:

Keeping Tabs

Have students track for one week how much they pay in sales tax on items that they purchase, plus other taxes that they pay. (For example, students with part-time jobs may find that taxes are taken out of their paychecks.) At the end of the week, students can find out how much they have paid that week to the government.

Name(s) _____

Go to: www.scholastic.com/profbooks/netexplorations/index.htm

Who Should We Bill for That?

Oops! Someone in the U.S. Postal Service sent you all the bills that should be going to the local, state, or federal government! Now you'll have to send them to the right address so that they'll get paid. Read the list of bills below. Then, use the information found at the links at the above web site to figure out where to send these bills. Draw a line from each bill to one of the three mailboxes shown.

BILLS

1 new bulb for the street light on Main Street

Salary for Motor Vehicle Bureau employees

Medical care for disabled veterans

5 new library books for the public library

Food and clothing for prisoners at the county jail

Salary for bridge and tunnel toll collectors

Interest payments on the national debt

3 new school buses

Salary for highway patrol officers

Scholarship dollars for students at a state university

Salary of air-traffic controllers

Funding for medical research

Go to: www.scholastic.com/profbooks/netexplorations/index.htm

Social Studies Math

Deeper in Debt... Or Is That Deficit?

Students use their research and math skills to figure out how much each American would need to contribute to pay off the national debt at various points in our country's history.

BACKGROUND

In 1835, Andrew Jackson became the only U.S. President ever to pay off the national debt and leave office with a surplus in the U.S. Treasury. Since then, the debt has continued to grow. In recent years, politicians have debated the benefits and drawbacks of using any budget surplus to pay off the debt. While some argue that paying down the debt is essential, others say that other priorities, like saving the nation's Social Security system, fixing the health care system, and improving the education system, should come first.

DOING THE ACTIVITY

1. Direct students to a dictionary to distinguish between *debt* (amount of money owed) and *deficit* (spending more money than one is bringing in). Explain that the national debt is equal to the sum of all the country's unpaid deficits, plus any interest payments that are due on it.

2. Photocopy and distribute page 45 to each student, student pair, or small group.

3. While some students look up information at the computer, others can use calculators to find out how much each American would have needed to contribute to pay off the debt in the years shown.

4. Ask students, Based on the chart, in what year was the national debt the lowest? Were there any years in which the size of the population decreased? The government has a fund to which people can contribute to help pay off the national debt. Would you be willing to contribute to this fund? Why or why not?

ANSWER

YEAR	NATIONAL DEBT*	TOTAL POPULATION**	PER PERSON PAYMENT TO CLEAR DEBT (rounded to the nearest cent)
1800	$82,976,294.35	5,308,483	$15.63
1850	$63,452,773.55	23,191,876	$2.74
1900	$2,136,961,091.67	75,994,575	$28.12
1950	$257,357,352,351.04	150,697,361	$1,707.78
1960	$290,216,815,241.68	178,554,916	$1,625.36
1970	$389,158,403,690.26	203,302,031	$1,914.19
1980	$930,210,000,000.00***	226,545,805	$4,106.06
1990	$3,233,313,451,777.25	248,709,873	$13,000.34
Current Year	(answers will vary depending on when activity is done)		

More To Do:

Graph the Results

Using graph paper, invite students to create one or more line graphs illustrating what they found out from this activity. Then, on the back of these sheets, have students write down three or more conclusions that they can draw from their graphs.

Name(s) _____

Go to: www.scholastic.com/profbooks/netexplorations/index.htm

A Big Budget Balancing Act

The chart below contains information about the national debt and the population of the United States in a number of different years. Click on the links at the above web site to complete the population and national figures. Use a calculator to determine what each person would have had to contribute to pay off the national debt for each year shown. The first one is done for you.

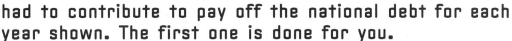

YEAR	NATIONAL DEBT*	TOTAL POPULATION**	PER PERSON PAYMENT TO CLEAR DEBT (rounded to the nearest cent)
1800	$82,976,294.35	5,308,483	$15.63
1850	$63,452,773.55	23,191,876	
1900	$2,136,961,091.67	75,994,575	
1950	$257,357,352,351.04	150,697,361	
1960	$290,216,815,241.68	178,554,916	
1970	$389,158,403,690.26		
1980	$930,210,000,000.00***		
1990	$3,233,313,451,777.25		
Current Year			

* According to the Department of the Treasury
** According to the U.S. Census Bureau
*** Rounded to the nearest million

Social Studies
History
Critical Thinking

Campaign Finance Reform

Presented with a number of dilemmas in campaign finance reform, students recommend their own solutions before finding out what legislation has actually been passed to deal with the problems.

BACKGROUND

Questions regarding who may contribute to a politician's campaign, to what extent, how these funds are solicited, and how they are spent, have been raised among politicians and government reformers since the earliest days in U.S. history. The first laws to deal with the problem were enacted in the mid-1800s. But every few years, when politicians and their financial backers seem to have found ways to work around them, the laws have had to be reviewed.

DOING THE ACTIVITY

1. Photocopy and distribute page 47 to each student, student pair, or small group. Read the facts on the worksheet as a class and discuss how students would have dealt with each problem.

2. Have students click on the links at the above web site to answer the questions.

3. Encourage students to share and compare their answers with actual legislation that has been passed.

ANSWERS

1. a) It made it illegal for federal civil-service workers to solicit money for their campaigns, and forced government hiring to be based on qualifications, rather than party affiliations. **b)** The Hatch Act made it illegal for federal workers and contractors to contribute to federal campaigns and put a limit on the amount of money individuals could give to a particular candidate. **2.** The Tillman Act prohibited banks and corporations from making political contributions to federal candidates. The Taft-Hartley Act made that ban permanent and extended it to unions, as well. **3. a)** The Federal Corrupt Practices Act established disclosure requirements for federal candidates, and put limits on candidates' spending. The 1971 Federal Election Campaign Act replaced the 1925 law and contained better enforcement procedures. **b)** Political action committees allow for voluntary contributions by individuals within a corporation or union that can then be pooled and legally contributed to a federal election campaign. **4.** Answers will vary.

More To Do:

Let's Make It a Law!

Based on what they've learned, invite students to suggest new legislative measures that might help to improve, in whole or in part, the problems that still exist regarding campaign financing.

Name(s) _____

Go to: www.scholastic.com/profbooks/netexplorations/index.htm

What Would You Do?

Click on the links at the above web site to read about the problems of keeping the financing of political campaigns honest. Using this information, answer the questions below. Continue at the back of the page.

1. In the mid-1800s, government officials threatened government workers with the loss of their jobs if they didn't vote for them in upcoming elections.

a) How did the Pendleton Act of 1883 deal with this problem?

_____

b) How does the Pendleton Act compare to the Hatch Act of 1939?

_____

2. In the past, large corporations would give lots of money to candidates that they liked. If elected, these politicians would often pass laws that benefited the contributors—whether or not these laws were in the best interest of the people.

How did the Tillman Act of 1907 and the Taft-Hartley Act of 1947 deal with this problem?

_____

3. During the Teapot Dome scandal of 1922, a member of President Warren Harding's staff accepted a bribe of $300,000 in exchange for leasing government-owned oil fields to the Mammoth Oil Company.

a) How did the Federal Corrupt Practices Act of 1910 (revised in 1925) and the Federal Election Campaign Act of 1971 try to address this type of problem?

_____

b) What is a Political Action Committee (PAC)? Why were PACs originally formed?

_____

4. People have argued that some laws dealing with the misuse of campaign finances are unconstitutional.

Do you think that any of the laws described above are unconstitutional? Why or why not?

_____

Resources

Books ⊙ Software ▯ Videos 🖱 Web sites

Teacher Resources

White House homepage
http://www.whitehouse.gov/index.html

History of the Federal Judiciary
http://air.fjc.gov/history/

Virtual Tour of the U.S. Government
http://www.virtualfreesites.com/us-gov.html

Schoolhouse Rock!: America Rock
(Disney Studios, 1997) This 30-minute video contains 10 of the original *Schoolhouse Rock!* short animated segments about U.S. government and American history.

Candidates, Campaigns, & Elections
by Linda Scher and Mary Oates Johnson (Scholastic, 2000). Contains election basics, ways to use newspapers and television to teach about elections, and more.

Bringing the Social Sciences Alive
by Frederick M. Hess (Allyn & Bacon, 1999). Ten tested, varied, and refined simulations that will enliven a classroom in grades 7—12 without sacrificing content.

Student Resources

Ben's Guide to U.S. Government for Kids
http://bensguide.gpo.gov/

Mr. Smith Goes to Washington
(Columbia/Tristar Studios, 1939). Share with students this fictionalized (and idealized) account of how the Senate works.

Ghosts of the White House
by Cheryl Harness (Simon & Schuster, 1998). Bored by the White House guide's presentation to her class, Sara is happy to be snared by the ghost of George Washington, who takes her on his own tour.

Jump Ship to Freedom
by James Lincoln Collier and Christopher Collier (Yearling Books, 1987).
A 14-year-old slave winds up at the Constitutional Convention in Philadelphia.

The Kid Who Ran for President
by Dan Gutman (Scholastic, 1996).
After collecting enough signatures to be placed on the Wisconsin ballot, Judson Moon finds himself on the official path to the Oval Office.

Meet My Grandmother: She's a Supreme Court Justice
by Lisa Tucker McElroy (Millbrook Press, 2000).
Courtney O'Connor and her grandmother, Sandra Day O'Connor, give readers a tour of the Supreme Court and explain how it functions.

So You Want to Be President?
by Judith St. George (Philomel Books, 2000).
In a fun, engaging way, St. George describes some of the good and bad points of being president of the United States. She then goes on to describe the personalities and quirks of some of the nation's former leaders.

Presidential Elections and Other Cool Facts
by Syl Sobel (Barrons Juveniles, 2000).
Describes in a fun-to-read way the process of selecting a president, and the order of succession.

How the U.S. Government Works
by Syl Sobel (Barrons Juveniles, 1999).
An easy-to-follow, fully illustrated explanation of how the U.S. government works by a director of the Judician Center in Washington, D.C.

A Kid's Guide to America's Bill of Rights: Curfews, Censorship, and the 100-Pound Giant
by Kathleen Krull (Avon Books, 1999).
Each chapter focuses on a different constitutional amendment.